To Carolyn
my Friend
For
Life

K Takra
Shine

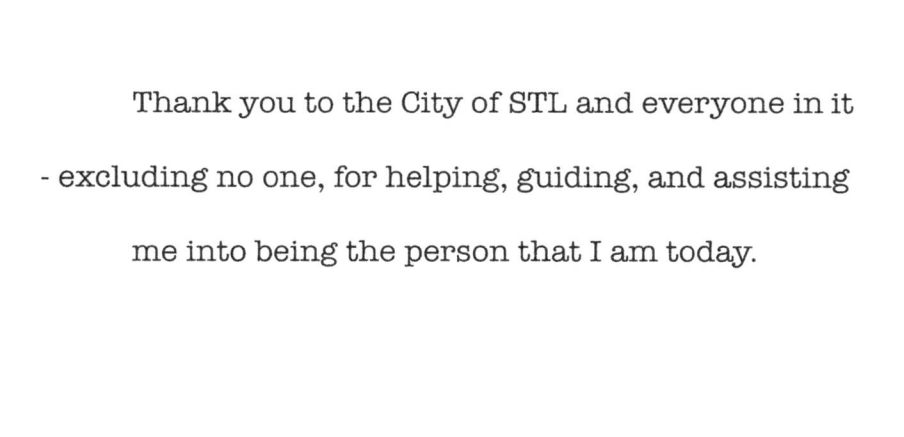

Thank you to the City of STL and everyone in it - excluding no one, for helping, guiding, and assisting me into being the person that I am today.

It's my story, the life of Richard "Shine" Rainey.

Peace, Love, & Prosperity

TABLE OF CONTENTS

1	Chapter 1: The Warm Up
22	Chapter 2: School Daze
35	Chapter 3: Changes
52	Chapter 4: Turbulence
67	Chapter 5: Off The Porch
79	Chapter 6: Kane and Abel
104	Chapter 7: So Far Gone
115	Chapter 8: Down On Grand
129	Chapter 9: Home Un-Sweet Home
158	Chapter 10: The Clean Up
164	Chapter 11: Still Going

The Warm Up

Okay, here we go - a story about one of the "Last Mohicans": a mantra that is used often and, in my opinion, of context. When I think about the Mohicans, I think of a battle to exist, survive and thrive. So that's why this story that you are about to read fits. Not only is it real, it's raw and authentic. It's my story, the life of Richard "Shine" Rainey. This guy is something else, I tell ya. With a nickname like Shine, you know he's got a personality that shines brighter than a star. He's got that charisma that just draws people in.

I was born August 15, 1963 in Chicago, Illinois. The phrase, "Summertime Chi" wasn't even a thought. Let me paint a picture for you, the times I was born in was tough for blacks. I mean during these times we still had segregation going on. I mean we had things like the Chicago Freedom Movement, the education strike, and the West Side Riots. We talking times when black folks were really in the thick of things, fighting for their lives. These were some of the Mohicans that I come from.

Check this out though, going back far as I could remember, I had to be about three years old. Growing up on the southside of Chicago, Englewood to be exact was rough. Notice I didn't say tough, because from the time I was born I was on a rollercoaster ride.

Now that I look back on how I was raised, I would have to say I was treated like a black sheep. I was probably about three or four when I first began to use my cognitive skills, because anything before that is a blur. All I could remember is living with a lot of people. It was an experience that was both chaotic and exhilarating at the same time. In our crowded household, there was never a dull moment. The constant noise and commotion became the soundtrack of my everyday life. The house was always filled with laughter, conversations, and the aromas of delicious home-cooked meals. Despite the occasional disagreements and conflicts, the love and sense of belonging were intense.

    Then things began to stick, once my father came to pick me up one day. It was mixed emotions because, up until then he was a stranger. Getting adjusted to my new life started off smooth. Little did I know these next moments would be a critical time in my development. Like I said, I was just starting to understand my surroundings and form bonds with those closest to them. For some, this transition may come naturally, but for me it was quite challenging. I wasn't approached in this period with empathy and understanding. Instead, I was treated as if I was supposed to already be on routine. My first few days I could feel the tension in the house. My mother yelled at me and my father consistently.

A few months into my new living arrangement, I learned that I wasn't an only child. So, here's the thing - my father has a bit of a complicated family situation. Turns out, he had a secret love affair that resulted in the birth of a not-so-expected bundle of joy. Yep, he has a bastard son. Think that's a plot twist, not only one but two. Being that we haven't spoken in years I won't make them nameless, instead give the aliases. Not just with them, but for all parties I had encountered.

One of my brothers, let's call him Tim, was the epitome of coolness. Always sporting the latest trendy clothes and effortlessly pulling off that "I woke up like this" look. He was basically the definition of a smooth operator. The other brother, whom we'll name Jake, had a different approach to life. He believed that he was superior to us mere mortals.

Tim and I, on the other hand, decided to take a different route in life. We embraced our innate sarcasm and saw the world for what it truly was - an ensemble of absurdity and irony. We took pleasure in poking fun at the self-proclaimed superiority of Jake, always finding new and imaginative ways to burst his metaphorical bubble. It became our mission, a quest if you will, to challenge Jake's sense of self-importance at every turn.

From light-hearted banter to intricately orchestrated pranks, every interaction with him turned into a delightful battleground of wits. Oh, how we reveled in the collective eye-rolling that came from our undying commitment to sarcasm. We built an entire world around our sarcastic banter. It was as if every word we uttered carried a hidden punchline, waiting to be deciphered.

It brought us joy to see the confused expression on Jake's face as he struggled to comprehend our humor. Little did he know, his self-proclaimed superiority was no match for our quick wit.

Now even though my brother was around,

which wasn't often, I found it to be my escape from my everyday living. When they weren't around it wasn't always so pleasant for a kid my age. Life lessons seemed like an everyday occurrence for me.

Back then, a lot of people may say that tough love was normal, and our parents did the best they could. Unfortunately, I believe that my mother was a lot harder than most. Before grade school began I knew I had already received a lifetime worth of ass whoopings. My father never really intervened so at this time I even thought I felt it was a bit much. I never thought they were unwarranted.

By the age of five or six I had graduated from the little innocent boy, to the curious versions of myself. See, I had started to notice the difference of my parents' moods and what they meant for me. My mother was the type of woman, I guess, who said she was going to have the life she wanted by any means. If it was one thing my mama was going to do was get the money. It's the epitome of what they call now "getting to the bag".

She used everything as an opportunity to try and live what she felt was the American dream. When it came to us as a family, we kinda lived like the Huxtables - so to speak. We never really missed any meals, and she made sure we had all the necessities.

She had a few hustles. One of her hustles she had for a long time was the gambling house. Now the gambling house introduced me to the dark side. The gambling house was a bittersweet memory. On those days, the preparation was hell. She would whoop my ass all day until the house was set up like she wanted it to be. Most times I would be the only kid in attendance.

See, my mama was like Ray from the movie "Harlem Nights". She used to set up her backyard like a hood casino and for me I knew that I would have some peace. Reason being, once she started to have her special drink, she was the nicest version of herself. Depending on how the party went, I might get that version of her for a couple days, up to a week.

One day, amidst the hustle and bustle of the neighborhood, a special occasion was unfolding. It was the annual neighborhood block party, and excitement filled the air. The streets were filled with laughter, joyous melodies, and the tantalizing aroma of delicious food. I remember sitting on the porch when a random man approached my parents flaunting a wad of cash. Standing back off to the side where a couple other people were looking on anxiously.

Words were exchanged, the man left and maybe fifteen minutes later he and the other gentlemen returned with a few cases of my mom's special drink. Just like that, the block party went from the street to my backyard.

Everything about this day was random. I forgot to mention on this particular day Jake's "bougie" ass had been dropped off unexpectedly. Surprisingly, he was actually cool. Usually when my mom threw her gambling parties, she would be prepared to host. Since this was a spare of the moment type situation, they were behaving out of character.

I usually wasn't allowed in the backyard during the activities, but since they didn't set up the coolers and stuff, Jake and I had to be runners.

Together, Jake and I hatched a plan. After we had made a few runs, we slipped away from the adults and made our way towards the fridge for Mom's special potion. We tiptoed cautiously through the house, unaware of the risk we were actually taking. We grabbed a can out the fridge and jetted to the bathroom. Once we both got in we locked the door, laughing chronically we turned the sink on to pretend like we were washing our hands.

This part was Jake's idea- me personally,

I had already grown immune to punishment, so I didn't quite care if we got caught. But the thrill of the mission and the fact Jake wasn't being snooty made it worth it.

We popped the top on the can and both took a gulp. The moment the liquid touched our tongues, an explosion of flavors erupted in our mouths. Bitter notes danced with the warmth of spices and a hint of something magical. It was like nothing we had ever tasted before. We felt an instant surge of energy, as if every cell in our bodies was awakened by this enchanted drink.

We finished the can and put it in the trash and walked back out as if nothing had happened. It wasn't long before we began to feel funny. Like I said we were no older than six. Jake began to throw up not long after we had the drink. With me also not feeling well, my mother's instincts kicked in and before we knew it, we could hear her scream to my father that we had drunk a beer. Sick and all, we still got our asses beat.

Not long after that, something unexpected happened that changed my life forever. My father, the vibrant soul who always brought laughter and joy into our lives, passed away. It was a shock that left my family in a state of utter disbelief and profound sorrow. He truly was the balance to the household. The house that was once filled with warmth and tranquility now felt empty and cold.

The familiar aroma of my father's cooking was replaced by a haunting silence that echoed through the hallways. It became a constant reminder of the void he left behind, and the empty chair at the dinner table that no one had the heart to remove.

In the process, I also formed an unexpected bond with my mother. Our shared grief brought us closer together, and we found strength in each other's company. We laughed, we cried, and we reminisced about the beautiful memories we had with my father. Life indeed changed after my father's passing, but amidst the heartache and uncertainty, I discovered the beauty of resilience and the transformative power of love.

My father may no longer be physically present, but his spirit lives on within me, guiding me to embrace life's challenges with strength and grace.

After my father's death, I noticed that my mother's aggression started to grow. It was like a wildfire spreading through her emotions, consuming everything in its path. She never was too gentle and understanding, but now she seemed to be constantly on edge, ready to pounce at the slightest provocation.

It broke my heart to see her like this, but I knew that the loss of my father had taken a toll on her. I tried my best to support her and provide her with the love and comfort she needed, hoping that one day her aggression would subside.

By the time I made it to grade school, I knew I was different. I just couldn't put a finger on exactly what it was. During school, I excelled in the curriculum, but I yearned for something more than an education. Well, I didn't know how to put it into words, so I acted out in class. I got hell all through grade school, the kids in my neighborhood for the most part went to public inner city schools.

Meanwhile, I had to dress up in this religious-like uniform and attend private catholic school. To and from school I found myself in plenty of scuffles.

Growing up wasn't always easy for me. I mean, sure, there were the bullies at school who would pick on me, but sometimes it wasn't just them. Sometimes, I had to deal with my own mother.

Now don't get me wrong, she had her good days too, but there were times when she could be a real handful. She would say things that would cut me deep and make me question my worth. Life was tough when the person who is supposed to love and protect you ends up hurting you instead. But hey, life's full of ups and downs, right?

Things weren't just verbal either, she had a number of tactics she used once my father's passing to make a man out of me. I remember one sunny afternoon, as I was returning home from school, disaster struck. I had found myself locked out of my own house with no spare key or any means of getting inside. Baffled and frustrated, I peered through my bedroom window, desperately searching for a solution.

To this amazement, I noticed a peculiar-looking envelope stuck behind the curtain. Curiosity piqued, as I swiftly fished it out. The envelope bore an intricate wax seal, intact and untouched. With trembling hands, I carefully broke the seal and unfolded the note. The note read, "go fight".

As I looked back through the window, I could see my mother standing there with her arms folded. Fear and determination coursed through my veins. I knew he had no choice but to initiate violence. At this time, like I said, none of the kids in my neighborhood I really had a relationship with - well - up until this point outside of them trying to harm me.

So here we go, I waited in front of my house with the mindset that it would give me an advantage. In my mind yea she wanted me to fight but there would be no way she would watch and let it get out of hand. So I waited and waited, and finally an opportunity came along.

A couple kids that I had run from numerous times came riding their bikes down the street. Now don't let me fool you into believing that I wasn't scared. I damn near was ready to shit my pants, because even though I wasn't a punk, I wasn't that much of a fighter either.

Before I knew it, things played out like a movie. Of course they saw me standing there all alone and when I say John Singleton couldn't have written a better story, because this here was crazy. They started out circling me on their bikes, talking shit you know. Outnumbered, I look back at my mother as if to say, "you can't be serious". With a blank stare she closed the curtains and left me out to dry.

Ready to get it over with I got to going back and forward with their boys jawing, until they eventually hopped off their bikes. Scared as ever, I swung first and connected, but that triumph was short lived. When I say they beat the brakes off me, they did me dirty. A neighbor ran them off, then brought me to my mother's doorstep.

Knowing my mother already knew what had happened, I stood on the porch in complete disbelief. I was heartbroken. My mother had sent me outside not only to fight but to be embarrassed. My mother had finally come to the door and let me in. She gave me a speech on how a mad man always takes his problems head on. I assume she meant well but that ignited something in me. For the next few weeks periodically, she would lock me out to fight. Some I won and others resulted in similar ass whoopings.

School Daze

Again, growing up was tough, not only physically but mentally as well. You see my mother did all these things raising me that seemed off, but being that it was all that I knew and her being my mother, I figured it was a way of life. So as I stated before I always knew I was different but couldn't pinpoint it. One reason I knew I was different was the schools she enrolled me in.

The first school I attended was a private catholic school. I found this out during the constant bullying I received en route. Now my route to school wasn't that long. It was actually across the street from where we lived. All I would have to do is walk through the gangway and I would literally be on the school grounds once I crossed the street. The only bad thing was all the kids that were bussed out to public schools would be there waiting on me.

During these times, everyone had to wear uniforms. They were very distinctive and quite frankly I hated them. Also at this time my experience with other kids had grown to be situational. I would rather much make friends, but I usually found myself alone or fighting. So safe to say I was a little awkward when it came to being with my peers.

Also around this time, lines were mandatory for everything. We had to line up to enter school, go to classes, water, and all. One particular day I was about the third grade when we had to do a play. For whatever reason, I was given the funniest character in play. I ended up being the grandpa. I mean they went all out with make up and wardrobe. They did everything they could to assure that I could pull off the old man look. If social media was around then in the late 60's, I definitely believe I would've gone viral for that performance.

After being so good in the play, I received props from almost everyone in my graduating class. It wasn't long before my name was buzzing in the school. From the teachers to the parents who saw the play, showered me with love and recognition. It wasn't long before the school bully wanted a piece of the kid with newfound fame. He was an older kid, and since we didn't have technology like we do now, things lingered on for weeks or until something new happened to overshadow the previous event.

It had been a few weeks since I starred in the play, but the hype around my role had yet to die down. I remember being in line to leave lunch and on our way back to the classroom we stopped at the restroom. On the way in, a few older kids were coming out but that wasn't abnormal.

It wasn't until I got all the way in did I realize that I was screwed. The school bully and I for the first time were face to face and alone. Before I could even turn around and try to get out of there, he grabbed me by the collar of my shirt. On this day though he didn't beat me up. Instead, he began to mock me, per se. He went on about how he didn't see the play and thought I should say a few lines. A nervous wreck, I found myself performing for him in the bathroom.

Being that we had to line up and do counts for everywhere we went, the teacher found his way into the bathroom and cut the hazing short. Boy, was I relieved. You know at this time I really didn't know much about fighting for real. Even though my mother by this time had made me fight a couple times. It still hadn't clicked. So the bully, now knowing who I was, began to seek after me for the next few weeks or so. I can't lie, sometimes I tried to defend myself, and then sometimes I ran.

For the sake of this next story, I'm going to call the bully Max. The oppressive heat seemed to intensify as children eagerly awaited their turn at the water fountain. In the midst of the chaos, I found myself at the front of the line, patiently awaiting my chance to quench my thirst. Suddenly, a mischievous boy wearing a tilted baseball cap and a sly grin approached the line.

It was Max, again known for his impulsive nature and knack for stirring up trouble, he brazenly attempted to bypass the line claiming innocence with wide eyes. My blood boiled, and a fire ignited within me. How dare he think he could deceive us all? Without hesitation, I stood my ground, ready to defend the order we had so patiently established. The fight had begun.

With a determined stride, I confronted Max, my voice resilient and unwavering. "No cutting in line, Max! We've all been waiting our turn, and you should too!"

Max chuckled mischievously, his eyes gleaming with defiance. "Why wait when I can just quench my thirst right now? Besides, the water fountain is within my reach. So, what's the problem?"

His words triggered a surge of adrenaline within me. I couldn't let him brush off the rules so easily. As the tension mounted, bystanders gathered around, their whispers creating a symphony of anticipation. All eyes were on us.

As we stood face-to-face, a battle of wills ensued. Pushing back my fear, I had summoned my courage and refused to back down. In this moment, it wasn't just about a line or a water fountain; it was about justice and fairness.

Without warning, Max lunged towards the water fountain, his fingers barely grazing the lever. But I was faster. Reacting with lightning speed, I blocked his path and firmly grasped the lever, preventing him from taking advantage of his impulsive judgment.

The crowd gasped in astonishment. Max's smirk faded, replaced now with surprise and maybe even a hint of admiration. Despite my small stature, I had proven that determination was a force to be reckoned with. With a newfound strength, I spoke with conviction, my words echoing through the corridor, "No one skips the line, Max. Remember, respect and patience are virtues we all must embrace."

Max still insisted on trying to get some water. We began to jockey for position and eventually led to us throwing blows. I don't know if I was that thirsty or fed up, but I gave him a fight he didn't sign up for. We ended up tearing the water fountain off the wall. They ultimately blamed and expelled me for destroying property.

Ironically sitting in the office waiting for my mother I was greeted with smiles. This was one of our highlighted moments because the whole way she explained how proud of me she was for taking up for myself.

It took her about a week or so to get me enrolled into a new school. Therefore I had to go to my aunt's house for the time being. That was my first taste of enjoying not going to school and doing what I wanted to do. My aunt wasn't as strict as my mother, but she also didn't have patience- so that was short lived.

My mother ended up enrolling me into

another private Catholic school. In this go around, school was slightly different. I remember being at the school for a couple years. Just like any other student I got into a few scuffles here and there, but I still didn't consider myself a fighter.

I had found myself being more focused and enthused with the schoolwork. I don't know if it was because I now had girls at my school and didn't want to be labeled dumb, or if I just really wanted to do what was right.

Although I still had a strong dislike for school. I must say that I had thought I found my place in life. Unfortunately, I ended up running into a few more bullies and that was all she wrote.

You see, for me to start a fight at this time, meant that you deserved it. I had grown to understand the position of bullies, and also the importance of taking up for yourself. Since I wasn't no longer what you could consider scary, it was just certain shit that I didn't let go.

So again I found myself dethroning the school bullies, this time though convincingly. Of course the last straw was with the country white boy. See it was fine when he was doing it to the black kids, him and his homeboys. The moment I embarrassed him, his father was at the school threatening to press charges.

I mean, I guess I gave them a reason, but I think it was more so my history. My mother was upset, because she felt that I was now the bully. She never really took time to listen in most cases, that is why my first expulsion was weird, but a good moment. Because I understood why it happened.

My mother made it very clear that she was not going to waste another dollar on my education. She enrolled me into public school. I did my last few months at the public junior high. Then things really changed gears once I went to high school.

Changes

Now before I even made it to school, I had had an eventful summer. With the few family members in Chicago that I knew, I ended up spending a lot of my days with my cousin. He was kind of like me, but I think from his perspective he was just a product of his environment. On the other hand, the trouble we got into was because of choices that I made. Even when I tried to do right, somehow and some way it was actually wrong.

So one day, not too long after we had got out of school, my cousin and I had done just about everything teenage boys could possibly do to not get in trouble. At this age, fighting was included in those activities. We had just come from the corner store. We never had any money so of course we either hustled the snacks or schemed and stole them. How we got the snacks on this particular day doesn't even matter. I just know that was our thing. Now what I do remember is it being hot as fish grease. I remember this because my cousin complained the whole walk home. In result, we ended up taking the short way home, a route we usually didn't take. Let's just say the boys down that way didn't play. So to take the risk of a beat down, it had to be hot.

We had made it halfway down the block, when this dog came out of nowhere. The barks at the time sounded like lion roars. Usian Bolt couldn't have caught us with how fast we took off. Once we made it off the block we no longer heard the dogs bark and or footsteps. We slowed down and eventually stopped to catch our breaths.

Thinking it was about to be a round for the chase, the dog came trotting around the corner. My cousin started to run, but I noticed his posture wasn't aggressive. I had learned about animals a little bit during the times my mother would make me read. I always chose books with a lot of pictures and very few words. Anyway, I managed to get the dog to run to me and obey a couple commands.

My cousin thought I was crazy for dealing with a stray. This wasn't no stray, he had on a collar which meant he must've got off his leash. We could've walked him back around the corner, but after that run and that heat I said fuck it, lets keep him. We took his collar off him and gave him a name. We called him Lucky.

On the way home we had discussed, well

I had convinced my cousin to lie and say that somebody gave him to us. The thought that my mother went with it and let me keep him was far-fetched. Once we made it to the house, she was standing on the porch waiting for us.

Just like I thought she threw a fit. "Hell no, take it back right now", my mother was as mean as she seemed, never really cursed so to get a "hell" out of her I knew something awful was about to happen to me. Then, Lucky shot up the steps and laid beside her, but before barking at us.

He had got to her, she took one look down at him in confusion yet still with a slight approval. As we approached the steps she gave me one last mug, told my cousin to have his mother come get him and went in the house. I sat on the front waiting for my cousin to be picked up and gave him a bath.

      The first few days of having the dog was a breeze for some reason the dog created some weird bond. Even though she made me go through hell and hot water to get some money to feed him, she loved his company. Time went by and Lucky went from my dog to our dog.

      She ended up developing these rules for Lucky and I ain't like it, you know. So creeping up on thirteen, I began feeling myself a little more. She had tried to whoop me for having the dog in my room. I was fed up by then so I snatched the belt and she never whooped me again.

      As I got closer to the first day of high school, It was like a switch had flipped in me. I no longer wanted to be on the short end of the stick. I started to branch out from my mother's wing and see what the world had to offer me.

One thing I learned quickly was that everyone around me, who were considered to be someone of importance, had similar qualities. They were either feared and or respected. Trying to understand the difference between being feared or respected didn't matter much to me. I just knew I wanted one or the other and or both.

Closer I got to the first day of school though, the sides began to play tug of war with me. I wasn't at the age where I could work yet, but I noticed that the first step to earning respect was to get some money. See, around this time, the color of your skin still dictated a lot of things we had access to, but as long as you had that green paper, it was like a pass.

      I started off going around my godfather who had his own barbershop and was doing pretty good. You know from what I could see he was very much respected. Everytime I would stop by, I would see the same guys hanging around talking shit and drinking. It didn't take me long before I noticed that even with the camaraderie and good feelings that being around them had on me, there was a feeling that kind of trumped them.

      It had been a few years since the Black Panther Party had made its mark in the black communities. Chicago, being one of the cities that some of its founders chose to put a chapter, it kind of started a snowball effect.

Upon arrival a few other organizations were born, and so did the jock for territory. These were the ideologies I had aligned myself with. You see, these men had given me an outlet to get some of my frustrations from at home out into the world.

Little did I know that these organizations would turn into what we know today as gangs. It started out as a brotherhood, you know. Even though these gangs caused a lot of destruction to the movement, at that time being fourteen it seemed cool to be a disruptor.

After I had been initiated into the brotherhood, they kind of took care of me. During the ruckus, I was able to find some order out in the world. I had slowly found what I felt like my purpose was, and just like everybody else, I wanted to be free. Not in the sense of a slave, but just freedom to be me.

This journey flowed right into the first day of high school, which from what I could remember was crazy. I had a few years at a co-ed school but none like this. Those last few months of junior high didn't prepare me for the world that I was about to enter. I remember entering the building and everything moving so fast. It was like organized chaos if you will. If you ever saw the movie, "Lean On Me" then you could almost get the picture of my first day. I mean it seemed as if the kids ran the school.

Now luckily I didn't have a normal first day, I wasn't considered fresh meat. I was just another student. Mostly because since I was affiliated with the gang life, people treaded lightly when it came to hazing.

Thinking back on it now, that was the introduction on the distinction of being respected or feared. At that moment in time I fell in love with the fact that I was more so feared than respected.

Now never did I consider myself as a follower, but you know when you considered hip, you just kind of did the things hip people did. Now when it came to right and wrong I never really learned which was which until I made it home and got the approval of my mother. Let me say this now, it wasn't too much I did around her or that she knew that was to her liking. So essentially I grew numb to trying to do what was "right' but more-so do things that I wanted to experience.

I mean, I don't know if you know what it was like for me, to hear and believe that I was loved, but to also feel like there was another version out there. A better version, at that. So, rebellious ways kind of got embedded in me without me knowing.

So check this out, my mother didn't like for people she didn't know to come to the house, so I never really had company outside my company.

Once my father died, going to see my brothers was also out of the picture. So instead of having them at the house I would catch their bus home and hang out for a while. This one particular day we went to my boy's house and his parents were gone for the weekend. An experience that I had never known. Having the house to yourself, with no supervision for that length of time was exciting to me. My boy was kind of a square so he was just kind of going with the rules left. Not me, I thought to myself let's have some fun. But before I get into this story I got to preface it.

Remember the story about me getting kicked out of school the second time? I didn't quite tell the whole story. See what had happened was, I didn't only beat him up, I had help whooping. The bully and I had been going back and forward in small exchanges. By this time though, I had already had my little posse. One of my close friends, his name I won't mention - as a matter of fact, I will keep all acquaintances nameless.

Anywho, I guess the bully called himself fed up with position locking in the school so he challenged me to a fight. Like I said I had a posse, but my close friend figured we didn't need to take any chances.

So we decided to get him to meet at the back of the school, and he did. When he got back there, he had his boys with him but when it popped off me, my homeboy jumped on him. His friends didn't help and that was kind of the end to his reign at being the school bully.

Like I said though, it was also kind of my last day at the school as well, so I could've been wrong.

Sometimes, I would get on his bus and walk home afterwards. This day after the fight we decided to make a detour where the older kids hung out after school. The older kids grew to like us, because we were smart with heart. It was a great combination for them to create ways for us to become entertainment. One day after we had been coming around for a few weeks, we had ended up getting some money somehow and buying us a joint.

At ten years old, we bought our first joint and got high for the first time. It was like a celebration for us. This was the true introduction to addiction and I didn't even know it.

So, now four years later I kind of became a pro with smoking. To be quite honest I probably smoked more than the adults. I never really had to buy it, being that the OG's would give it to me as a form of payment - a lot of the time for all the bullshit they had us doing. So, as we were chilling in his crib I found his father's ashtray hidden on the porch.

The reason I say hidden is because it was tucked behind two boots. It had a little piece left, and unconsciously I pulled the lighter out my pocket and sparked it. My boy went crazy. He just kept screaming how his dad was gonna kill him. Now the funny part was my boy was built like his mama, and his daddy, lets just say my boy had the advantage in the weight department. So, If he was anything like my mama, and he was anything like me, I figured there was no reason he should be worried. Then I remembered he was kind of square, so I understood.

I eventually got him to settle down, giving him a credible lie. He eventually ended up being my smoking buddy after that weekend. His father didn't believe the lie, instead he pressured my homeboy to tell and they ended up smoking with each other. I guess he won in the end.

Hold on, see that brought back memories I almost got ahead of myself. I was letting y'all know how my household forced me to want to experience things, maybe at the moment if ever I should have tried. So it took me a day to talk him into smoking, but once I did, boy did he loosen up. Now up until this day I had yet to have a female for company. Out of all the things I got into, this one mission I hadn't quite had the opportunity.

So on the last day of the house to ourselves, I went to his house early that Saturday and had a few girls that I tried to call. That didn't work, we walked to every park in the distance searching for action. Y'all when I tell y'all it took a whole year for that mission to be complete, to the point that's all I could really remember doing freshman year - trying to get some female company.

Turbulence

Sophomore year, Sophomore year.

Yes, it was so monumental that I had to say it twice. The beginning of the year was different because I had a shift in focus. The gang activities were getting old, and I had found a new challenge. Ironically the same activities I was trying to shy away from is what got my first piece of action.

On the last day of freshman year, there was a big ass brawl, and I ended up protecting "Jasmine" who became my first girlfriend. She fell for the macho me. So in result she played the role of a bad girl. We had spent much of the summer together and her father didn't approve of us being together. Now he didn't live in the same house with her, but she was a daddy's girl. She, of course, rebelled and her mother worked the mid shift so it fit my schedule perfectly.

See, my mother ended up giving me a curfew over the summer. Her rule was if I wasn't in the house by 8pm I couldn't eat. She never said not to come home, just not to eat. I went hungry for many nights thinking it was a game.

Fast forward to now, we just got our first quarter grades. I was getting by, but I really wasn't sold on the education part of school anymore. I was at the point where I felt like I learned enough at home with Majorette Payne. Jasmine was so stuck on me she did whatever to get a thrill. I also think she acted out because her parent separation was new for her.

We ended up skipping school more often than not. She started smoking with me and we started having sex. Then that ended up getting old quick. I found myself skipping school and just going to drink and smoke in the neighborhood, I was back hanging with the gang.

It was early into the year still I know because it was still football season. After the games the school would have a couple rivalry fights with nothing major. You know it might last through the middle of next week depending on school. So, one night after a game I got into it with some guys. My boys who didn't go to school were there but, as I did, they reacted in self-defense.

A riot broke out that night like I've never seen. I mean I've seen brawls, but when I say I don't believe it was a person that was there that didn't fight. It was to the point where you really couldn't tell who was on what side. Just whoever hit you, you had to hit back.

The next day, I got to school, and they called me to the office. When I got there it looked like an overflow of the nurses offices. Everyone including me was scratched and knotted up. They went in one by one and after maybe two hours it was my turn. I had been in the office so long, they had eventually brought me lunch. So I had to wait while the staff and I ate.

Upon entry to the assistant principal's office, she didn't waste any time. She questioned me about the incident the night before. I tried to lie about it, saying I had nothing to do with it. I thought since so many people had got down, it was no way possible they could know. Unfortunately, I was wrong as two left shoes. She let me finish, then she let me know that the whole school had snitched on me. She said the rumor was that I started the fight with some gang members. Being that they said it was gang related, they said they were forced to expel me.

So here we go again, another situation where I am just being a part of my environment and doing the things that were normal to us. Somehow, some way all my situations were weighed differently. My mother had come once again to sign paperwork and shit. So I knew some type of punishment was coming.

Surprisingly this time though the punishment kind of worked in my favor. She switched tactics and somehow got me into this performing arts school. All the kids had some type of talent. I didn't really have anything to offer, but I gave it a shot. I tried the band, theater, and even the choir. I didn't like too many of them. I think I stayed in theater the longest, simply because I thought it was dope to act crazy and get a laugh and not be in trouble. I probably stayed focused at the school for maybe three months then I was back skipping school.

I would find myself in all types of places. It had got to the point where I didn't even go inside the school. So right before the holiday break you know testing time, I had come home right before curfew and my mother was waiting for me at the table. She had this look as if I was late. So I jumped the gun trying to lie about where I was. She stopped me cold turkey. The truancy officers had been by the house and spilled all the beans.

The rest of the semester was pure hell. She had taken the door to my bedroom and put it on the back porch. She changed shifts and all types of shit to make sure I stayed at school. Had to be one of the most belittling moments of my life at that time. Could you imagine at sixteen having your mother come check on you in the middle of class?

I ended up finishing out the school year underneath her supervision. Coming up on another summer, I remember staying out too late. I may have missed curfew by an hour. I ended up sneaking in the house. When I say sneak I mean creep, because like I said I was never actually locked out. Now knowing the rules of the house, especially after curfew - after the year I put up with I don't think none of that shit mattered. I was close to summer days with no school, fresh off a completed booty call. I was feeling good and before I called it a night I told myself I was going to eat.

So I took out the food from the fridge and made myself a plate. I even took the risk of warming it up. I don't think the sound was loud enough, but the ready noise might be. So, I even stopped the microwave before the time ran out. Before I could even sit down good, I heard a noise creep up on me. As I turned to see what it was, I was startled by the blast from a gun.

Yeah! My own damn mother shot at me. I had been in the streets and doing all types of shit and the first time I was shot at it was by my damn mama. She missed by a long shot, I don't know if it was on purpose or not. But I know once I came out of shock, I went to my room and went to sleep.

When I got up the next morning I could hear Lucky barking. I got up and went to check on him, she had given him the plate of food I had made for myself. The rest of the leftover was in the trash and of course she was gone.

That was kind of my last straw with being in the house with my mother. I had begun to find my exit strategy. So from that day I made up my mind that I was going to find ways to think for myself. In my mind, I was ready to be the man I felt I was.

Summer was in full effect and I was growing in every way possible. Lucky and I had just gone about everywhere in the city making friends and shit. So it had crept up on the 4th of July weekend and of course my mother wanted to find a way to rain on my parade.

Since the 4th was on a weekday they were having the parade on that Sunday morning. My mother had to work, so just to make me mad or keep me from going she told me I couldn't take Lucky. I took to that very much.

I ended up leaving the house without Lucky and heading towards the parade. I may have gotten two or three blocks from the house then I thought about it. I wasn't gonna let her dictate what I did with my dog. I understood her authority, but she just did shit to piss me off. I was tired of being shitted on, hell besides school I literally worshiped the ground she walked on. I just felt I deserved to be happy too. So, the whole way home I reasoned with myself.

When I got back she was gone to work and Lucky was sitting in the back with no water, and no food. It was like she was trying to kill him. I was glad I came back. I kept an old milk jug to walk around with when I took him with me. I filled it up and we walked to the parade.

Once we got there everything fell into place just like I thought. The energy and vibes were high, and everyone was in their red, white and blue. It was literally one of the best parades to date.

I stayed longer than normal, because everybody had to stop and pet Lucky. I met a lot of good people because of him that day. The sun began to set, and as it did we found our way back home. There were still plenty of people out on the streets, drunk and amped up from the fireworks. I wasn't worried about the curfew because I had ate plenty at the parade and then my mother was working a double. There was no way she was going to beat me home.

Literally a block from the house, I walked into some type of domestic dispute. Until this day I don't who, what or why, but a fight broke out and then shit got hectic. Lucky began barking and being protective, but then gunshots rang out. I took off running with Lucky when all of a sudden the leash tugged.

The crowd had dispersed and blew past me. I turned around to see Lucky had been struck by a bullet. I stayed there as he gasped for his last breath. I took his leash and collar from around his neck and let him die in peace.

That walk home was dark and lonely. It was like I couldn't win for losing. One part of me was like damn, my mother knew best even in her fucked up ways. Then the other part of me said hell he was gonna die regardless in the heat with no water and food. So instead of trying to find the silver lining, I figured out a way to soften the blow.

When I got home, I put the leash back on the pole like he ran away. It took my mother until the next morning once she woke up to notice he was gone. She stormed my room in this frantic panic as if she was heart broken. She went on screaming how somebody had stolen Lucky. I played along with her, crocodile tears and all, hell my tears were actually real. She didn't know it, but I knew what had really happened.

A week or so goes by and I guess she went and investigated who stole the dog. How I don't know but she found out I had taken him to the parade. She kicked my ass for the first time in years. It was like she had more love for him than she did me. I never forgot that beating.

Off The Porch

My junior year for high school was about to start, and I remember I was supposed to go get my schedule. I went, but it just didn't feel right as I stood in the line. I got all the way to the front then just left.

When my mother got home from work I was sitting at the table eating and when she asked to see my schedule, it was at that moment I let her know that I was no longer going to school. I had expressed to her that I had learned all that school could teach me and I no longer felt I needed it or the issues it brang. I had been to five or six different schools and I was over it. She gave me an ultimatum and it was either work or school, but in order to stay in her house I had to be productive.

For the first time in my life I felt heard and actually felt like my life was about to be on the up and up. I ended up getting my first job bagging groceries at the local market. Having a job gave me a good sense of purpose. I took pride in being able to see a reward for my work. I never had any problem when it came to work ethic, it was just finding what interests me.

I had been working for about two or three months before my mother called herself teaching me another lesson. So one day after work, my mother had packed up all my shit. I was confused because she had told me that as long as I got a job, I was good. Of course I was fucked up about all my shit being packed up in boxes. We had words back and forth, then she explained to me it was time that I learned now on how to be independent.

She had signed some paper that legally made me legally responsible for myself. As a result, I was able to move out and get my own place.

You are talking about an exhilarating feeling. It had to be one of the proudest moments in my life. I had my own job and house. At seventeen, I was doing something grown men couldn't do. It was at that moment where I began to feel like all my troubles were paying off.

My first day in my new spot I began to learn a lot about taking care of a household. The first thing I learned was that it cost a lot of money to furnish it how I was accustomed to living. My mother was nice enough to let me keep the covers and the mattress so for a couple weeks that's all I had.

I eventually worked to get my furniture piece by piece. Second thing I got was a tv. I didn't know how to cook so there was no need for dishes besides some bowls. My lifestyle quickly turned to work and noodles everyday.

It didn't take long before living paycheck to paycheck got old. Then my hand was kind of forced you know to get into the wrong shit. So I found myself stealing from time to time. I never physically robbed anyone, but if it was something of value laying around that I could get off quick for a few bucks, I got you.

One day I was on a mission to hit a lick and ended up running into one of the guys from the set. He was a couple years older than me, but for some reason he always hung around the young cats and gave us game. I never learned his real name. Everyone in the hood though knew him as Buck.

Buck had a reputation of being a hot head, but I had never seen it for myself. So when I ran into him at the corner store while he was hanging out, I noticed he had a pocket full of money. Now it had crossed my mind to rob him, but I didn't own a gun. If I had one I doubt I would've got him still, just because that wasn't really my motive.

So instead I ended up asking him where he worked. Green to the game, I aint even peep he was working the block. He had shown me some weed, and said he was always clocked in.

He assumed I was a custo. For those that

don't know, "custo" is short for customer. Being an avid smoker, he was right, but with pockets hurting like they were, I was more interested in the selling. I asked him to put me on and that was what he did. He showed me the ropes, and I was a quick learner - like I've always been. Before I knew it I had been rolling in dough.

    I would work the store by day and then catch people in the parking lot by night. It got so good that I was able to furnish my house with all the necessities, and still entertain my women on the weekends. Jasmine and a few other stragglers would come by from time to time.

    When I say I was the man, it was nobody my age doing it like me. I was on a full high.

    Ironically, the separation from my mother

was just what I needed. The relationship remained strange but this go around she handled me differently. It was like she already knew it wasn't shit she could do to me. Not physically anyway, but when it came to verbal abuse that in my opinion got worse. I went from being son, to nigga, and some more shit. I took it on the chin though because it didn;t change the fact that she was all I knew, had, and loved.

After a year of living by myself and finding out about what the world had to offer, I had found myself comfortable in the direction I was going. Buck and I had formed a well-oiled machine getting to the money. I still had my grocery job, but I was no longer a bag boy, I had been promoted to stocker.

After I got my raise, I was able to up my purchase amount from Buck and I quickly got to the point where I no longer needed to sell, so I eventually slowed down until it got to the point where I stopped completely. The money was damn good but I couldn't get with the constant standing and waiting after a shift. I was just good at it and fell into the trap because I was in need.

Buck and I was cool so he thought of an idea where he could take over my post and his brother would watch his spot. That worked out for about two weeks and you saw it in his moves. Buck went from being lowkey Buck to splurge Buck. His whole wardrobe changed, walk and everything. If you ask me he brought way too much attention to himself.

Then to be standing at the store everyday and all day was a no-no. I never thought about it, but I overheard one of my managers speaking on him.

They were trying to see who he was and why he was there. Knowing the answers to both I chose to mind my business. I even stopped speaking to him in the eyesight of the door.

On a ride to work one day, after he had bought a new car or whatever, I can't remember if it was a El Camino or an SS, but I knew it was clean. I had explained to him that maybe being there so often was good. I even suggested repositioning himself.

He didn't take my advice and it wasn't a month later when he was cornered by parking lot security and the cops. That beautiful ass car I believe was the tipping point for them white folks. He ended up going to jail and they ended up finding out we were associates. I got fired and the cycle of rising and falling began again.

I ended up finding out about a connect on some tree, and I made shit shake in my little building. I was able to stay afloat for a while. I found a paper route, and they provided the bike, so I used that on Sunday to fund my smoking habit. Slowly but surely the young women I was dating were falling by the wayside. Either getting ready for college or on to something new.

It had only been four months since Buck went to jail and I had been writing to him the whole time. I received a letter letting me know he was coming home in a couple months and he had big plans.

Those two months flew by as we communicated the whole time. I didn't have a car so when he got out I had no way to get to him. I got a call one day and it was him saying, "homie, I'm coming to see you stay at the house".

Kane and Abel

"Honk, honk". I heard as I sat in my room. I peeped out the curtain, and what do I see? Buck in that pretty ass old school vehicle. It's a shame I can't remember the type of car. Don't worry though, you are about to find out the reasons why, and it's just not because of old age.

So I get outside and greet my homie, and see he's swole as shit. We get to kicking it like he never left. This time though it was me trying to put him on. Trying didn't get too far, he had already converted. You know they say men go to jail for parking tickets and become a muslim for protection. My homie had been in for four months and was devoted.

He had changed his name to Nasir and some

more shit. First day out though, so I expected that. He swore he was going legit. I was happy for him, even though he had gotten me fired. I had yet to find another job due to my educational background.

Buck, Nasir, whatever his name was, meant every word he said. He had got a security job fresh out. I remember us cracking jokes as he was going through the training. He graduated from the academy, and upon completion they gave him a pistol.

I've always been a supporter of the ones I cared about. That's just how I am. As he always did he pulled up on me honking his horn. Excited as a three-year-old in a candy store, I'm walking over to his car, and I mean I'm cheesing hard. I'm happy for him.

I get up close to the glass then I see him with his pistol. I was thinking it was to show me, but nope. This man, with the window still up, waited til I leaned in, then shot me.

This dickhead who I called my homie, had the nerve to shoot me for no apparent reason. So here I am, adrenaline rushing and all running down the street. I had to have a guardian angel, because where I stayed on the corner wasn't too far. I fucked around and ran right into the path of a squad car they threw me in the backseat and sped off.

Now I'm in the back, adrenaline on a thousand because I'm still conscious, I just knew I didn't want to die right then. So I guess the combination of my body being in shock, the adrenaline and fear all together had me on one. I remember the cops going through my pocket and getting my ID. Then I heard one say "he's not one of them". I don't know what that meant, but what I did know was they took me to the ER and dropped me off.

Man look, when I say I wish I was making this shit up. I promise you I do, but I ain't even faking it. Man, the hospital was so full they didn't even look concerned about what was going on with my eye.

I did manage to get checked in, but hell, I left with my eye fucked up and all, so I got myself to another hospital. Just in the nick of time too, because soon as I hit the door I passed out.

When I had awakened I was fresh out of

surgery, and everything was a blur. I knew my mother was sitting next to me because she wore this distinctive perfume and it seemed like it was right on top of me. Then it was followed by her stanking ass breath.

I hadn't actually seen my mother in four months, so to soon be turning nineteen, with one eye I was bitter to have her by my side. Then all those feelings went away to hear her call me son again. The doctors came in and explained to me exactly what was going on.

They had let me know they were able to stop the bleeding, but I had to stay a few more days as they did routine checks since I still had a bullet fragment in my head. My mother didn't stay long as she went back to work so I spent those days alone.

The only visitors after that were the cops coming to let me know they had caught Buck. I had the option to press charges but, snitching just wasn't me. The state picked up the case since he used a registered working firearm.

I went back to my apartment, broke and unemployed. Recovery was rough, it was an everyday reminder that for the rest of my living days I was going to be considered disabled. Thoughts like that got to me, but then here I go receiving some mail from a law firm I never reached out to. All the while, they were trying to contact me for a settlement. Since he used his work gun, to keep me from suing the company, they reached out and offered me a million dollar settlement not to press charges against the company.

Funny that thought never crossed my mind. One reason being because I didn't know you could. Nineteen, disabled and a million dollars come across the table , who wouldn't take that. I accepted the offer and from there in my mind my worries were over and done with. Sitting there alone, almost down to my last I was straight because I knew it was nothing but a waiting game.

My first check came within a few weeks. In preparation for it I went and did all the tests to get my license. At the office I ended up running into my old friend from high school. It had been a couple years since we last hung out and his energy was different.

After leaving the DMV, we stopped and grabbed a bite to eat to catch up and shit. Grown now a lot of things were talked about, but one thing that stuck out was that he sold cars. The money I had just got was burning a hole in my pocket. What's fucked up though is that he was out of inventory at that moment.

Back in motion, I sat at the crib and chilled most days, I eventually learned how to cook. My mother charged me for cooking lessons. Surprised? I didn't think so. I began to learn quickly because my mother was an opportunist. From experience though I learned all mothers were in some form or fashion. So I never thought too much into it.

After finally healing up, I got back to trying to live a normal life. Getting a job wasn't my main concern since I had more money rolling in from my disability than I had ever had. The neighborhood was starting to change for the worse. I mean crime was getting worse, and the streets roamed with many people with no purpose. It was like a city of lost souls was forming.

The Black Panther party and all its positivity had been halted with penetration of the government. So, the gangs ran amuck. Having one foot in and one foot out of the game, I did find myself in some activities I'm not proud of just by hanging around. Idle time at this moment was very detrimental.

Having nothing else to do to buy time, though, the block is where you would find me most of the time. If I wasn't smoking and drinking while talking shit. I was out somewhere laid up with one of the women I would run across. Outside of Jasmine, making a commitment to women never really came to fruition. It was mostly hit and quit type situations, then I was on to the next.

Cell phones weren't around like they are now, we mostly used pagers and pay phones. So part of the reason I used to go to the hood was because I knew somebody was always by the pay phone, and most likely if I received a call somebody would tell me. Part of my routine was pulling up and calling my home boy from grade school. I would call everyday to see if he had run across another car.

For a couple weeks straight, I would call and he would say he just sold his last one. I had started to get pissed because I knew damn well he knew that I was looking for wheels. So one day instead of telling him I'll try again tomorrow or later I asked him where the lot was and that I just wanted to stop by from time to time. He was cool with it, in fact he ended up telling me to come by his house and he would take me.

He had moved to the westside of the city, a part of the city I never really went to visit. The south side and west side locals were in a big feud for a few years now. It was literally two separate worlds. I needed a car, and figured if my square ass homeboy was good, then I should be as well.

So check this out, we made it to this old run down looking house. It was hell of a lot of cars on the street looking like they had been stripped and parts sold. In fact, the street itself looked like it was starting to be abandoned in general. There were a couple saleable cars though.

We had to catch a couple buses and walked

a great distance to get there. On the way he stopped and made a few calls to what he said was his business partner. As far as I knew we were good to go. So here I am standing at the front of this house with a $5000 check in my pocket. We entered the house and the first thing I saw was a group of people sitting around waiting. It gave me the impression that they had been there for the same reason I was there, to buy a car. So I sat there and waited as well.

Meanwhile, I watched each one of the people sitting with me head to the back one by one. As I continued to wait, time went by and I thought to myself it's taking an awful lot of time just to go get a title. Instead of continuing to wait, I looked for my homeboy to see what was taking so long. Coming to find out everybody that was in the house we're sitting in this back room.

Now as I got closer to the room, I began to smell something that I have that I had never smelt before. It wasn't strong but it was an acquired smell, so here I am being nosy. I knocked on a door. My friend comes to the door and tells me he couldn't find the title, but if I wanted to sit and chill, I could. So that's just what I did, I sat, I waited, and then I got curious.

So I asked him what the hell are y'all doing back here. He proceeded to tell me, you know, just getting high. Now at this time I have been getting high for years and I had yet to smell anything of sort. Hell, to be honest from the looks of it I had never got as high as it seemed they were getting at the time. Again, being an inquisitive mind I asked what y'all smoking it can't be weed.

That's when he said no man not at all we are on a better trip. The room we were in was kind of like a den, it was attached to another side-room where they were actually making the drug. This was the first time I was introduced to crack cocaine. Being that my homeboy seemed to enjoy this high, I said fuck just let me try.

After my first hit of the rock, it took me on a trip to the moon. I'm talking about a fast ride, I'm talking about one or two hits and I had been higher than I ever was before. Before I knew it I had sat there for almost two days getting high and waiting on the title. It wasn't until I looked up and all the money I had brought with me was gone before I noticed how long I had been over there.

The friend never came back with the title so I took it upon myself to leave and come back a few days later once my next lump sum came through. I took a little more money than the last time I went, and rode the bus all the way to the spot. Now it never bothered me to call my homeboy because I just assumed that he would be there.

My second time arriving, and I don't even think I asked for the title or about the car. Once I got inside they had brought the session from the backroom to the front so I ended up spending a couple hundred dollars and hung out. This became my routine for the next few months. I had tried smoking weed after that, but the high wasn't strong enough so it didn't take long before the rock was my preferred choice.

Once I got hooked it was kind of too late to stop. I found myself shortly after receiving a few payments from the payout back down on my luck. In a few months, it had to be about six months max. I had a full addiction. So here I was at nineteen with my own spot, and being a millionaire (so to speak), but I was a flunky.

The addiction began to really take over and then I started doing things that was uncontrollable, and out of character. I didn't know it then, but looking back now I had kinda grew this "don't ask don't tell" like persona.

When I got around family members, or people I knew that didn't party, I would put on this act as if I wasn't using or had a habit. If you ask me, I think I was kind of in denial of who I had become.

The drugs for me was just a hobby. I didn't see it as an issue or addiction.

The installments of my money had slowed down, I think by now I had received like seventy-five thousand of the money, but I had smoked it all up. Crazy part is I had yet to pay my rent either for a couple months. I always was a smooth talker, but when you have an addiction it seems like your stories become more extravagant and somewhat believable.

So, with my disability and shit I persuaded the office that I was going to have the money, I was just waiting on the deposit. They dealt with me for as long as I could. After being about six months behind, I guess they had had enough. I had come back with a couple of my smoking buddies one day and my door had an eviction notice on it.

I remember reading the options I had and the date or whatever. One option was to pay the balance in full by the due date or be out by then. I don't know why, but I let my buddies talk me into letting the spot go. The bad part about it all, I had just received a lump sum of cash, and had the money to pay. Instead I pocket the money and we grabbed everything of value, then hauled it down to the smoke house.

You remember though the whole reason for me linking up with them six months ago was to buy a car. Now on this same day, is when I found out they actually were selling cars, but not the car entirely. It had all started to make sense. They were the ones stripping the cars and selling the parts to get high.

For some reason, after I had got evicted and started going from house to house laying my head my money slowed all the way down. So much to the point I had eventually sold all my valuables to support my habit.

One day, while I was out trying to support my habit I ran into my cousin- the one who had helped me steal Lucky a few years back. He had cleaned himself up, and found a way to be a law abiding citizen.

By now this cat was kind of out of the bag about my habit. My mother had banned me from the house, she had found out that everytime I came around something was missing. No lies told there though, I had definitely been by a few times and stole from her purse and sold a couple of her valuables. I think I took a couple rings she never really wore and a nugget chain my dad used to wear.

My cousin saw right through the act I was trying to portray. We talked for maybe two hours. That day, he fed me well, but the withdrawals was on my ass. I couldn't go too long without getting my fix. Cuz wasn't judgmental, so he helped me get my drugs for the day but before he did, he suggested that maybe Chicago wasn't the place for me anymore. His words verbatim, "cuz, you ever thought about moving and starting fresh, Chicago gone kill you if you stay".

Moving away from home never crossed my mind. You see at this time I felt like I still had control over my life. I still was able to get jobs, and when I came to work I always got praise for my ethic, but since that check hit my hand, the drugs had trumped any responsibility I may have had at the time.

Once the money dried up from the case, so did the party bunch. Everyone started to go their separate ways. Sharing the rocks was no longer sufficient. I had grown numb to seeing smoker overdose, and some more shit. The lifestyle never bothered me.

Shortly after the conversation with my cousin, somehow I had found my way back to my mother's house. She had needed me to sign some papers for her, the exact reason I can't quite remember but I knew it had to deal with her trying to get some money.

So during the conversation with my mother,

she blurted out some shit that had me puzzled. In a casual manner, she asked me if she thought adopting another child was a good idea.

Now even though I got high, and I lost one eye by now, I still had all my marbles.

So you know, being the only child for 20 years, her saying another child threw me off. So I asked her "another child, who was the first"?

Y'all, do you know this woman had the nerve to say "You.". When I say all the emotions running in me come out at once. At that very moment I was broken. I had so many questions and of course she had all the answers. I couldn't believe it, this whole time I had been calling this mean, conniving ass woman my mother all to find out we had no relation. Hell, I wasn't related to no one I thought was my family.

She ended up letting me know that my biological mother gave me up for adoption, and upon finding out my father chose to come get me at three. She couldn't tell me who my biological mother was, so I don't ever believe I even met the woman.

It was at that very moment that I knew my cousin was on to something. I know it might seem strange, but despite everything that happened in my life I still had love and trust built with that woman, but in less than thirty minutes, twenty years had been shattered. I reached out to my cousin, and talked to him about it and that's when he suggested he heard that Saint Louis was a great place to start over.

I had waited a month or so after the news was brought to me that since I was adopted, to make a decision, and once my mind was made up, I got together the little belongings I had chosen to make the move.

So Far Gone

My cousin was a real one, for taking me to the train - ready to embark on this new journey. By the time I made the move though, I figured going to St. Louis would be the place where I found peace. Up to this point I had found out that all my beliefs were built on lies and deception.

Once I put two and two together, I ended up figuring out that my mother's doing was based on our true relationship. She ended up telling me that she couldn't have kids, so, that's why my father came and got me because she always wanted a family.
So instead of adopting a kid, he thought getting me would be best.

Once he died she wasn't recognized as my

legal guardian, they never married. Basically, the state was gonna take me, but she kept me and they gave her a check until I was seventeen when she signed away her rights.

The train ride wasn't that bad, but those were the thoughts that raced through my head the whole time. So, knowing that I was on my way to an unfamiliar place- with no family, or any friends felt good. Even though I was born and raised in Chicago, I felt that moving to St. Louis was the same. The only difference was it had been lying and abusing me for the last twenty years.

After sitting for six hours, I had finally made it to my new home. Once I made it out of the station, the feeling of relief took over. See for years I had been hiding who I was, or the things I felt, because of how

I was raised. The things I witnessed. It never dawned on me that I was being led wrong.

So here we go, my first day in this foreign place. I call it foreign because I had never been outside Chicago before. So everything was brand new for me. I mean everything. Even down to the aroma in the air.

When I got off that train and walked outside, I kid you not, it was like I had walked into a bakery. The air smelled like fresh rolls had just been baked. Y'all know the smell I'm talking about!, You know that smell when you go to Shnucks or Kroger and walk past the deli and bakery!

That smell.

So I was dropped off downtown St. Louis,

and at the moment everything seemed fast to me. It was as if I was the only person around that didn't have a clue. I probably walked a couple blocks back and forth trying to find something to eat, which I eventually walked inside this nice ass hotel and asked around. The hotel ended up being the Mark Twain. I learned of a few spots to eat, since they were so helpful and nice, I ended up staying there. They let me pay up a month in advance, so that's what I did. Then for the next thirty days I roamed as far as I was comfortable.

    It didn't take long for me to get situated and comfortable in the city. Things were so different from back home. In a short period of time, I felt safer than I've ever felt, and the people were way nicer than in Chicago.

Now you all are probably asking yourselves about the addiction. Rightfully so, and so was I. I had brought some rocks with me from Chicago. Enough to last me a few days. Luckily I was able to stretch it out about a week or so. Even though this was supposed to be a fresh start, the rock was the one Chicago habit I couldn't shake. As I got down to my last I had told myself that I was going to at least be a functioning addict. I wasn't going to drown in this brand new city.

A month into moving the habit had begun to slowly but surely take over, especially once I ran across some other users. On one of my routine walks roaming the city I fell upon Swans. Swans was a commercial cleaning company, as long as you had an ID to show proof of age, you could get hired. I walked in and out with a job.

The job was pretty cool. They paid pretty okay for the work we did, and it kinda became a gift and a curse. The job took me all over the city so I quickly started to learn about the city limits and what it truly had to offer.

One of our main areas we worked was out in Chesterfield. Now, Chesterfield was an area that has always been considered off limits for certain types of folk. Not in terms of working class, but when it came to living. Yeah, if you weren't in a certain tax bracket, you probably didn't stay that way. It's safe to say that there weren't that many blacks out there at the moment.

I quickly found out that in Chesterfield, not all the white folks walked the straight and narrow path. On lunch break I would go to the McDonald's nearby and get me something to eat. I had been going so often that I formed a relationship with the manager up there. She was an older lady but she looked damn good for her age. She grew a liking to me, you know. When I came in she would take care of me and then one thing led to another.

While on lunch one day, she kind of got comfortable with me and we ended up talking about life, and getting to know each other quite a bit. She ended up inviting me out to her spot and we kicked it a few times.

Little did I know she was a rock head too. So once I found that out we became thick as thieves.

I had stopped staying at the Mark Twain, and moved to an all men hotel. It was like an extended stay for those who couldn't afford regular housing.

So I had paid up a month and shit but they had strict rules that women and kids couldn't stay overnight, so that was short lived.

In the midst of the rocky living situation, I ended up quitting Swans and working at McDonalds. It became part of the deal I had with the manager. She was able to get me a little apartment for little of nothing out in her complex. So, I moved to Chesterfield and focused on becoming a functioning addict.

I held the McDonalds job down and another little cleaning job on the side. Even though the money was coming in, handling my responsibilities never clicked. I wound up losing both those jobs due to the fact I had too many no call, no shows. After payday it was always party time. For days I would go missing and show back up as if nothing happened.

That led to me finding a few other small jobs that didn't pay that much, but I fell into this trap of dealing with women- who I thought were good women. But then again, when you are dealing with someone with the same habits, no structure could ever be formed. So, thinking I was doing the right thing I had few women over the next few months to a year I found myself taking care of. Not because I was in love or anything, but because I felt that it was the right thing to do.

I mean, the trips on the drugs were fun, and the sex was great, but when funds were low and the urge for another hit took over, things always got extremely toxic. Even on drugs though, I just knew it was certain things you just didn't do. I never physically abused women, but I took an awful lot of abuse.

    I ended up losing every job I had in Chesterfield, and it wasn't long after that my name was shot in the area. As a result, I ended up losing the apartment and once again I found myself homeless. I tried staying out of Chesterfield and roaming the area, but the police ran me out from that way. The cycle of Chicago living was now spilling over into St. Louis. After making my way back downtown, I ended up coming across a shelter.

Down on Grand

So the first time I was introduced to the street "Grand" I stayed in this all men shelter called, "The Harbor". It was located right there on the Washington and Grand intersection. When I got there, man! I know it wasn't technically mine but I felt like I was at home.

I ended up meeting a few good brothers who had been around the block a few times. They helped me out a lot. They showed me a couple places down off Grand where we could go get a meal and some clothes. As far as I knew back home in Chicago, if you were homeless you were just shit out of luck. You had to fend for yourself. Not here though, so even in my lows, St. Louis was teaching me how to have faith.

I had stopped working for the most part, and because in all actuality I wasn't hurting for money, I just had to play the waiting game with the checks. I was able to get a PO box close by for my mail. The only mail I was receiving at the time was my monthly check.

As the checks started rolling in I began to befriend people from the city, men and women, who didn't judge me or my habits. Most were users, those that weren't for a good period of time I was able to fool, and or, hide my extra curricular activities. That began to grow on me so I eventually only hung around those who wanted to get high. One of the women I began hanging with introduced me to this church.

I found peace in going to church, even much

so that I joined the singles ministry. This turned out to be one of the best decisions for me at the time. Reason being, it was helping keep me from focusing on the rocks. I met quite a few women in the ministry. Most who had such a great relationship with God, that they considered me bad for their image.

The few women I was able to trick, ended up being young, and you know how that goes. The only reason they found interest in me was for the money and sex. Before I knew it, I had thrived on this cycle for about a year or so.

Once that got old, I kind of left the women alone. I never swung to the other side of the fence, but I had learned that even though the women here in St. Louis were cool, I figured that my best bet was to coast through keeping my addiction to myself as much as I could, and continue to try and be productive.

It had been a minute since I worked a real job, so to get back in the flow of things I ended up strolling down Grand and seeing a few help wanted signs in the window. I had begun spending most of my time in the area anyway so I figured the best thing for me was to get a little job down the street from the shelter.

One of my first jobs down this way I started working at the McDonalds down on the riverfront. It was different from the one I worked at in Chesterfield- when it came to the amount of traffic, and type of people I ran into down there.

I ended up meeting this older guy I used to see from time to time come in and eat. I found it strange because he used to watch me while I work. One day, I mustered up enough courage to ask him about his inquisitive stares. While doing so, he applauded my work ethic and said that he had also seen me around. He inquired about my skills and schedule and ended up giving a card to come see him. It took me a few days to ponder on what had happened. After talking to one of the homies at the shelter, they told me that the card and man may have been my ticket out of the shelter.

So I made it to the spot on the card, just so happened it was a cleaners on Grand. I showed up and he was happy to see me. The old guy greeted me as if he knew me his whole life. He showed me a couple things about the business then offered me a position.

It was under what I was making at McDonalds, but he paid cash and it was weekly just like Swans.

For me, that beat out the riverfront. I did what I could to work both. For a while I did good, and what I meant by good, I went sober. Not completely, but it had gotten good to the point where I only needed a hit in between shifts, and on off days I celebrated.

After about three months at the cleaners I ended up getting a raise, and it was like the rocks knew when to call. Again, I had a motive to decide on two jobs or one.

I can't lie, being a productive citizen despite my flaws was finally paying off. I had been in St. Louis about four years now, and it was around the mid 90's- the city was really beginning to "pop". When I say pop, I mean in all kinds of ways. So Anheuser-Busch was taking off like a rocket, and when it came to biscuits, Pilsbury was the frontrunner.

With all this being at our disposal, the city was growing at a fast rate. With the city growing, it meant great for the economy, this being on both sides of the fence. About the same time at the cleaners, the clientele grew and this is when shit began to get rocky. Along with the raise came more responsibilities. I wasn't shy to work, but like I said when it came to my growth and development, it was like the rock would call for calmness.

Adding delivery as an option definitely increased the amount of business for the cleaners.

But it also turned out to be one of the cons for my position. The cleaners was a family business, which means that I was the odd man out. I had to find out the hard way because I never got a chance to drive the car. Yet, they gave me all of the walking distance deliveries.

On top of all that, we had to split the tips -in which I knew we didn't get an even cut. I spoke up about it and they played me like I was crazy. From there I understood exactly what it was. I gave it a month to die down. While on a delivery, I had to walk longer than usual, causing me to pass one of my duck off spots, you know.

I had a few alleys throughout the area that I would post up in and get my fix, and be out of the way of being seen or noticed. Most times while out during the day, I didn't want anyone to know. Not even the other junkies. I had got that good with hiding my habit.

Out of frustration I stopped and got a hit, the remainder of the way I was cool. I got to the door, made the drop off, and received a tip. Before I left, the customer had asked me about one of the employees, who happened to be one of the sons, who did deliveries; but he always drove. I let him know they sent me because he was backed up, and that was that.

On the way back I was coming down from the high. But like I said, when that rock started to call, everything around me seemed to crumble. I had made up my mind that when I got back I wasn't going to give the full tip. I stopped on the way, got change for the twenty, and kept ten.

When we broke down tips at the end of the night, I had no problem with my share. Hell, I ended up doing that on the next few deliveries. I had already pocketed enough for about three rocks. When I left that night, I felt like I had finally figured out how to even the playing fields. It went on for about a week, and turned out to be a great resource of income for my habit.

One night when it was time to break down the tips, the owner switched up the routine. He counted all the tip money in front of everyone, broke it down into three evenly, and then passed the money out to the sons.

I reached my hand out last, assuming I was

next and the strangest thing happened. Instead of giving me my tips he passed me a separation notice. Come to find out, they had been calling behind me checking the tip amount. Once again, the greed behind getting a fix got me caught up.

So I lost that job, but at least the money I pocketed they let me keep. The only thing I hadn't lost at the time was my PO box down at the post office. If anybody back home needed to reach me they would send mail, but I never got much mail.

Years had gone past and I had damn near worked at every spot on Grand. Of course my habits in some way shape or form made me lose each one of them. It was either no call/no shows, and then some of them I simply quit after I saw my first check. My last job, I got fired because I was caught smoking on the job. I was down bad by then.

I had started losing side teeth so it was kind of hard you know to keep hiding it. Most places just started accepting me and giving me a chance because I had a great work ethic. I was also cheap labor, word got around that I would take money under the table. Since I just wanted enough to stay high, I didn't complain.

Anyway, this job didn't believe in paying under the table. So once they fired me they were so upset that they didn't even give me my check, they mailed it to the PO box. So I had to walk ten blocks to get my check then another fifteen to get what I needed. When I made it to the post office my check was in there, but it wasn't the only thing.

Inside was a letter from my cousin. Upon opening the letter, I found out that my mother had passed away. The letter was back dated a month so I had missed her funeral and everything. I walked those fifteen blocks and I spent every dollar I had and got high.

Home Un-sweet Home

I was back in the city of darkness; it took me a couple of weeks after reading the letter to get enough money for the Amtrak. Even then the rocks had won. Anyway, my godfather picked me up from the station and took me to the house.

When my mother passed, it hit me that even though she didn't show it in an empathetic way, she really did have love for me. I hadn't seen or talked to my mother since the day she told me I was adopted. Yet, I returned home to a house and some money. Lord knows I needed both. My godfather gave me a job down at the shop sweeping and cleaning. It was just supposed to be temporary until I got myself a better job.

Being back home was bitter sweet. Especially being in the house after not speaking to my mother for so long. Being confined to the same walls where I had so many unanswered questions got the best of me. So many memories filled the house. For the first few days, I took time to take everything in. I had started to learn that with every beating came a lesson that I used later in life.

Just like it was supposed to, my time at the barbershop had ended. I didn't get a job, rather I started to live off the money I had. Being back in Chicago, my mind raced with questions about who I was and where I belonged. And that happened everywhere I went.

I eventually started back smoking weed, even after I smoked about a zip of it, it didn't quiet the noises. I found myself back on the rock. Along with some money and crib, she also left the car. It didn't take long before I lost them all.

It started with the money, of course, I burned through that in a few months. Then, it went to me selling all the valuables out the house. My godfather ended up coming by one day and seeing what I had done. He also saw that the taxes hadn't been paid, and the house was in jeopardy of being taken. He exploded and I understood why. But I have to be honest, even during his rant, I was high as a kite. Nothing phased me.

After all, I had lost the car and the house, he still opened his shop doors to me, and let me stay in the back room. His only rule was that nothing came up missing. With a habit like mine, that was damn near impossible. But he would give me a couple dollars before he left to help ensure that didn't happen. In retrospect, I guess he said if he couldn't help me quit one habit, he could at least make an honest addict out of me.

My godfather's best friend was a pastor. One Sunday after church he had a fish fry and I was invited. This is where I began to put vision with purpose. My godfather had shown great empathy by asking the pastor to pray for me. Then they kinda put me through a boot camp.

I hope you remember when I spoke about trying to figure out the difference between respect and fear. At thirty now, I was able to appreciate it more. Respect takes you a long way. One who is respected knows how to display respect. My godfather and the pastor showed me that. They knew exactly who and what I was, but they never judged me. Instead, they coached me on how to be self-sufficient and productive.

    Every Sunday, I would meet at the pastor's house, and he taught me how to shine shoes. By the end of his classes I knew how to shine shoes, but also repair all types of shoes. Once I learned all the tools my godfather agreed to let me work down at the shop.

    I got so good with the business he ended up gifting me a shine box and showing me a blueprint to follow. I followed that for about six months. My business was booming, but when it came to my lifestyle I still hadn't had nothing to show for it. I had done all I could do in Chicago. I was ready to go back to the place where I considered home.

Fresh off the Amtrak once again, back in the Lou this time I came back as a businessman. I'm back down on Grand, I brought my shine box and the blueprint my godfather gave me. This time though I also came free from shame. I was at the point in life where I understood who I was, and I was no longer trying to hide it.

I had tried going back to The Harbor, but after being gone for two years, I had found out that they had closed down. I then ended up down at Mother Theresa's building. The energy there was lively. Some of the guys I met while being housed there ended up being great friends with me. Once I got settled into the shelter, I took off with my shine business!

You see, my approach with the business was to target places where a lot of traffic formed. My top spots were going around to the nearby salons and barbershops. It was like taking candy from a baby. Being back home, I learned outside the hairdo, and the next most important thing was the kicks.

I started with the shops I was most familiar with. I would first go into an establishment and speak to the owner. Once I ran my spill with the owner, I would extend my services to those who worked there. On top of that, I took donations instead of giving a set price.

Leading with that, I was able to build clientele. I had worked at a few shops and salons on the regular. It wasn't long before between these shops I built a good enough rapport, to the point they would stand outside and look for me.

Previously, there was one shop I used to go to, that really helped me out. This shop showed me mad love. Ironically, they had a shoe shine rack set up in the corner of the shop. We ended up working out a schedule where I could come in and set up between certain hours. Before I started shining in this shop, I didn't have too many nicknames. You know, nicknames meant people fucked with you or you are important.

Check this out. Everyday I came into the shop they had one barber who would yell out "watch out now, here comes "Tricky Ricky". Man I used to fall out laughing. I got a kick out of that name. Y'all maybe wondering how I got that nickname. Besides the obvious, it came with a funny story.

Since I came back, I had been coming to the shop to get business for months. I was technically a regular there. This was the shop where I cut my curl off. Y'all might not believe me but I had it all the way up until I left for Chicago.

Back to the story at hand though. From time to time, there would be dead days in the shop. So, instead of sitting around, I took walks. Sometimes when I come back, I'd have a friend with me. And sometimes I wouldn't. So, the guy who used to cut my hair asked me one day why I'd be gone so long. So you know, I told him I'd be out looking for business. Shortly after he asked, I must've shined a couple shoes and made a few dollars. I was still working on donations. In between time, this old babe I used to fuck with, came walking by. She ain't see me but I saw her. I shot out of there, and I was probably gone for about thirty minutes.

When I got back, they ended up asking for some change. It was early so nobody had any ones. So, they would holler at me like "Aye Rick, let me get them dollars I got a five for you."

Mind you I sat over there quiet because I knew I ain't have it either. Hell, I ain't got a dollar to my name. So I responded "Man I'm broke as a joke." Puzzled as hell, he responded "Man I just tipped you for my shoes." Now he was correct but I couldn't tell him what I just did.

Even though I didn't want to tell him, it was meant for him to know. A movie writer couldn't write a better scene. Before it registered in my brain, the clucker was standing in the window screaming, "thank you, Ricky". For some strange reason she had came back around and blew my whole cover. Man he must've looked at me and died laughing. He just kept saying, "got damn Tricky Ricky". From then on that became a running joke, but it was true. They knew I got high and they knew I tricked on women.

The shop was a safe place so as they got to share stories, so did I. I shined inside that shop for years. I mean I outlasted a lot of the barbers. My boy who gave me the nickname, left and got his own shop. I never made it to his shop but he always came back and showed me love.

Now don't get me wrong I spent time in the shop but no longer than 3 hours a couple days out of the week. So, Shine had time to roam the city.

I started where I felt most comfortable - down on Grand. I started at the cleaners. The old guy had gotten sick, but was happy to see me. Ironic here, I was with my own business, and finding purpose. I was back here offering a hell of a service for the same thing I was fired for, tips! It was a full circle moment.

I shined his shoes so good that he extended his clientele. This is when I learned my worth, and how to price to different types of clientele. He also added shoe shining as a service. We came to an agreement but that didn't last long at all. I couldn't shine at his spot because the wife complained about the smell. So, I would take them to the shelter and back to the shop to shine them.

One day Tricky Ricky went on a mission and never went back. I fucked around and forgot about the shoes entirely. I went back to the cleaners days later for a pickup before I went to the shop. The customer and owner thought I sold them for drugs.

I was fired right on the spot, again, only this time I didn't actually work for him. The feeling was humiliating. I made it all the way to the shop, only to find the shoes hanging on the shine box. I shined the shoes and took them right back to the cleaners. I was embarrassed because I didn't sell drugs. Drugs were the reason I had no recollection of them. I was still able to save whatever face I had left, and then also let them know that the days have passed for me to steal for a high.

By this time, a year or so had gone by, and I had formed a relationship with every spot that I was fired. I had a steady flow of work. Stressing about money was no longer a factor. I had grown so widely known around the area. I had developed a new nickname: Shoe Shine. But most just called me "Shine" for short. I liked the name, because it meant that I had aligned with my purpose at that moment in my life.

That shine box was the gateway around the city for me. I had made my way so far that I had ended up working with almost every district in the city police department. When I say the whole city of St. Louis welcomed ol' Shine with open arms, that's what I mean.

Maybe you're thinking, if business was so good then why couldn't Shine get ahead?

The answer is that I was hooked. I mean,

hooked so bad that I really couldn't tell you which way was up when I didn't get a fix. While in Chicago I had learned that I was a father. And I was given an ultimatum for the opportunity to be around my daughter. I tried, but even then, I couldn't shake the habit. It was like when I didn't have it, I was a different person. It had a stronghold on me. It was like my body couldn't function unless I had it.

The money and the rocks was what kept me going. St. Louis just became the canvas, and the people were my audience and rather they cared for the picture or not, they respected the craft.

Like I said though, the shine box took me into places where normally someone with my habit wouldn't be accepted. For example, when it came to the police officers, I used to go down to the headquarters and set up outside. Before and after their shifts, they showed me mad love. Not one time did I get run off or treated like a junkie even though I was.

I didn't stop there. At night, the drugs would keep me up so I really didn't get a lot of rest or sleep. I had learned where the popping spot was from sitting around at the shelter and drinking with the guys. Wherever they promoted on the radio, I would show up and work the line.

My approach was so well put together, even the young crowd rocked with me. With the young crowd I really made some bank. Especially with the patent leather Jordans. And when it came to restoring Jordans, I used to have the parking lot on lock.

The thing about it though was the process took just a little time. So after maybe five or six shoes a night, I would slow all the way down. On club nights I would charge ten to fifteen dollars, and make close to $100. On most days after getting two or three rocks I'd end up with enough for some food, and maybe a drink.

My routine became pretty regular for years, as times changed, so did the game. I was still thriving as Shine, but the money had slowed down. The major factories had been gone for a while now, and the effect on the economy really started to show. It's crazy how much things could change in a decade.

With times changing and money slowing up not just for me but for everyone. The competition had spiked for everyone. Now all of a sudden you had junkies everywhere on hustles, shining shoes had become a big then. Street hustles in general, from panhandling, magic tricks, selling fruit, socks and a whole bunch of other shit.

Then when it came to finding your drugs, the prices went up, and the dealers became way more cutthroat. You had to be careful who and where you bought from now. Now when it came to me and where I got my fix, I never dipped too much from where I felt comfortable.

If I wasn't downtown, I would be heavily present on the northside of Saint Louis. I even went as deep as Florrisant sometimes. But the rest of the city never really pulled me in. I would shine shoes on the west side every now and then, but not once did I shop.

When I got down to the Salvation Army, I kinda got wind of the places where I should and shouldn't be. Then I remembered how it was back in Chicago: the south side stayed south, and the west side stayed west. So I took the stories and the experience from back home in Chicago, and just stuck to it here in St. Louis.

Roaming the city, though, I did stumble up on a lick. So I got a side job cleaning the AT&T building. Using my charm and wit, I was able to befriend someone who worked in the building. Thai was by far one of the most interesting experiences I had. This had happened when I was still faking as if I didn't smoke.

I would clean by day, and for a year straight, that person taught me how to draft on computers. A position opened up and he recommended me. I ended up getting hired, then somebody hated and asked for my credentials, and my cover was blown. They had figured out that I had no educational background, so I was let go.

Now besides losing any and everything I loved or valued, my life didn't create too much excitement. What it did create for me, was peace. The fact is that everyone was so welcoming, they were at peace with my lifestyle, in which I ended up getting too comfortable.

When I would get my fix sometimes, I'd find myself on walks to sightsee and talk to myself. When I was high, even though it was my escape, it also became my way of therapy. Fucked up I know, but I remember one time I had got high and was having a conversation with my mother. You know, asking her all the questions I wish I would've asked, and playing out the answers I felt I needed to hear at the time. I had to be tripping out because the police ended up flagging me, and found a rock in my pocket.

They locked me up for the night and that was my first time going to jail. Since it was my first offense, I was able to self-bond out. They gave me a court date. I missed that court date, fucked around, and went to shine shoes at one of the district's like a dummy. Then they locked me up for the bench warrant.

I ain't have a job, and since all the officers knew me when I went to court, one of them spoke for me and the judge gave me a provisional release - instead of the 30 day jail sentence. It's just another example of how St. Louis, and the work I put in over the city, repaid ol' Shine.

I'd be lying if I said I wasn't spiraling downhill at this point. It had become so common for people to get the services I offered now, and the once popular fads had changed, when it came to the newest styles. Maintaining them became so much harder.

I had worked all up and down Grand. One of the provisions for the charges was that I had to get a job, or work a hundred community service hours. So, I went back to every spot I worked and tried to get my job back, or work for free. This was the first time that the city didn't help me out. I hadn't burned my bridges with many of them on that level. If I did, they wouldn't have let me shine in front of their establishments.

It took some time, but I kept shining shoes. One night while shining some shoes in the back of The Best Steak House, the owner came out and saw me working. He let me finish as he stood and watched while smoking a cigarette. Out of all the spots on Grand, I had yet to work at this location. He called me over and asked if I wanted to make some money. I said yes, of course, and asked if it was a job offer. He quickly said, "no. I just wanted to see if you would take cash for a cleaning opportunity."

I assumed that he meant the whole restaurant. As usual, I jumped the gun thinking about just getting some money and ended up being on the grill -the filthiest and greasiest part of the store. Now, they had a place to shower my wardrobe, and it wasn't deep enough to be fucking with the cleaning supplies and grease. I had already agreed to it, even without knowing compensation. Anything twenty dollars and over, I would take it. For a job like this, though, I was thinking at least one hundred - a night.

The original owner, rest his soul, paid me twenty dollars a night. Another time where I was conflicted, I knew damn well that the job should pay more than twenty dollars, but I had a case and needed community service hours. So, I took the money and the job probably took me four hours every night. I was making five dollars an hour, we're talking real junky prices. On the back end, I had him sign for ten hours a day of volunteer work. After a week and a half, the ball would be back in my court.

Time goes on, and the steak house, I must say, has been holding me down ever since. I kept taking the petty money, then I ended up shining his shoes, and then his friend's shoes. I eventually got to hustling daily out the steak house, and from different hustles I would leave with a hundred or close to it; I was shining shoes and cleaning windows by day, and then the grills at night.

In between every shift, I made sure I was able to take a break for some hits. When the sun fell, there was no reason for me to be at the steak house. I had a cut off time for my services. The owner didn't want any extra transactions after sunset because he said it caused more risk for robbery. So since I would have to come back in a few hours, I would either go to the shelter or it was some project 'round the way where all the homeless people hung out. Sometimes I would take my box over there and get the hustlers right. Other times I would just be out doing my thang.

One night on the way back, I got flagged again by the police for drunk and disorderly conduct. I was talking to myself, having another one of those therapy sessions. What it actually was, though, was a cry for help. I did another night in jail, this time was just a misdemeanor, no judge was needed. I had to pay a fine, luckily, I had made the eighty dollars and didn't smoke it that night.

After consistently cleaning the windows and grill for a year, he started to pay a little better. My pay went up to fifty a night. I had picked up some more regulars down the street north side of Grand, so I did frequent late night runs for them.

On the way to make some money I popped a tall can. I had the brown paper bag around it, but got flagged anyway. They searched me, and this time they found two rocks on me. They had called it in on the radio, and once they read my name, someone responded asking about the box.

The officers were shocked that a bum like me was known and respected in their brotherhood. The banter went back and forward in police jargon. They took a step back, and let me finish my beer. So I did, they even let me take me and put my box up. Finally, they took me to jail. I was a two-time offender. I sat in jail over a week and it was the worst feeling ever. The withdrawals was a mother fucker.

When I got to court I stood in front of the

judge, and the judge gave me a speech that I needed to hear. You see, this was the same judge that gave me a break last time, off the strength of one of his peers. So, a year later was a slap in the face to everyone. The judge looked at me and said "Mr. Rainey, everything in me is saying give you the maximum sentence of twenty years". Hearing that damn near made my knees buckle. Instead, he gave me another chance. Instead of sending me to jail, he sent me to Job Corp.

The Clean Up

Normally the cut off age would be twenty four, but since I lost an eye my disability, an educational background qualified me for the program. I was by far the oldest one there when I arrived. During the program, you really didn't have too much contact with the people on the outside. We lived on this enclosed campus and only got specific times to talk. I didn't have too many people to talk to, and no home to go to so I was cool.

The hardest thing to do was get over the drugs, I went through so many phases. The first few weeks was the worst. Being the oldest persona and background, I was given my own room. I remember one night going through it so bad, that I damn near overheated. Being bawled up, ass naked, on a cold floor was one of the scariest moments of my life. There was plenty of long nights that I spent in chills, vomiting, and more. The program lasted eighteen long months.

The real test began. Back when the temptation was real for me, and I was faced with the choice of using drugs again. Once I left the Job Corp, I didn't make my way downtown. The Job Corp helped me find a job, but it was a temporary position and once I was let go, I didn't receive any callbacks.

That forced me to go back down on Grand, even though I was staying in Walnut park. In Job Corp they gave you a bi-weekly allowance, so I had saved up a pretty penny. It almost took a year for me to get a real appetite. Then, they awarded the students who finished with a lump sum of money.

So, between that and the temporary job checks I had enough for this house that was rent to own. I really wasn't trying to own it, but then here come these people loaning me thirty-five thousand dollars for the house.

In less than a year of completion, I was still clean and my reward was being able to buy a house. So, like I said, since Job Corp only helped with initial job placement, I needed something productive to do. The original owner for the steak house had stepped down and passed it on to his children. I had built up a great rapport, so once I returned, they all welcomed me back with no hesitation. This time, I wasn't getting paid under the table.

Then one day working there, it hit me, I was exactly where I needed to be. My mind was no longer foggy and everything was starting to come together. I was cleaning tables during a shift and ran into an old friend from Chicago. A lot had changed between the both of us since the last time we seen each other, but some people and things you never forget.

He ended up working at this school back home and one thing led to another. I'd be damned that he had contact with someone who could reach my daughter. We talked for hours and he promised me that he would help me out, seeing what he could do to bridge that gap.

A year went past and finally my prayers were answered. While at work, a young lady and her daughter walked in. Have you ever got a feeling in your soul that just filled you with joy and peace, that you had no choice but to cry? If not, I pray you feel it at least once.

      Before she even introduced herself, I already knew. Meeting my daughter and grand baby gave me the push I needed to survive until this day.

Still Going

I have been going strong ever since the day I met my daughter and grandchild. Years have passed, and I can't say it's been easy, but what I will say is that it's been a clean ride. I've been to the doctor a couple times since then, and to be honest I haven't heard anything good. One time, the doctor told me to get all the use out of my soldier, because he was soon to stop stepping. I was fucked up about it, but then again I was cool. Tricky Ricky worked his mojo.

When I look back, I lived three four lives in one lifetime. On the surface people may know me as an addict, but only if they knew I smoked up more money than most people touch in a lifetime. That, including the cash from my accident, plus the value of all the homes and cars I lost.

I had a habit, but damn, I lived pretty good. During the most recent trip, the doctor told me I had a bad heart. But like I said in the beginning, this was a story of one of the last Mohicans.

The crazy part about life is that even in your darkest days, it prepares you for your brightest future. You see, my whole life I yearned for certain material things and answers. During every stage, everything seemed so incomplete.

As a kid, I was handicapped because I wasn't given an option. I was born and raised without a choice. Then, I got older and thought the answer was loyalty, that led me to making bad decisions to prove myself worthy of reciprocity. All I wanted was the same support and love that I gave out. As an adult, I wanted understanding. I got that. I wanted direction, and I got that too, but not in the ways I needed. See, not everything you want, you will receive like you need; and that's what I learned, I should've been taught.

In my struggles I learned to be around people who benefitted on the necessity side, more than those for the wants. I also learned to apply what I learned to prioritizing my life. Going to Job Corp reinforced the discipline that I needed. Those lessons my mother taught me, I needed. It hits different when you realize the reasons why.

Sometimes I never came to any realization why. But when it's all said and done, I love my mother, because if she wasn't who she was, I would've been dead a long time ago. I may not have had the strength to leave Chicago if it wasn't for her. Until this day, she is part of the reason I'm still going right now. For everything I've been through, I'm grateful.

I would say the end, but I can't, 'cause I'm still rolling like a champ.

Peace, Love & Prosperity

Made in the USA
Monee, IL
21 June 2024